SIGN
LANGUAGE 2

D1438416

SIGN LANGUAGE 2

More Travels in Unfortunate English

T | TRAVEL
The Telegraph

Aurum

SIGN LANGUAGE

First published 2012 by
Aurum Press Limited
7 Greenland Street
London NW1 0ND
www.aurumpress.co.uk

Copyright © 2012
Telegraph Media Group

The moral right of Francisca Kellett,
Natalie Paris, Jolyon Attwooll and
Oliver Smith to be identified as the
Editors of this work has been asserted by
them in accordance with the Copyright,
Designs and Patents Act 1988.

All rights reserved. No part of this
book may be reproduced or utilised
in any form or by any means,
electronic or mechanical, including
photocopying, recording or by any
information storage and retrieval
system, without permission in writing
from Aurum Press Ltd.

A catalogue record for this book is
available from the British Library.

ISBN 978 1 78131 038 0

Compiled by the team at
Telegraph Travel:
Senior Editor: *Francisca Kellett*
Contributing Editors: *Oliver Smith,
Natalie Paris, Jolyon Attwooll*

10 9 8 7 6 5 4 3 2 1
2016 2015 2014 2013 2012

Design: Transmission
www.thisistransmission.com

Printed in China

CONTENTS

INTRO DUCTION

When *Telegraph Travel* first tentatively called on readers to send us their photographs of the poorly translated, rude, or simply baffling signs they had spotted on their travels, we hoped for a handful of emails at best. The response was little short of phenomenal. And, where we expected the deluge to eventually slow to a trickle, four years on we still receive around 50 submissions a week – not to mention countless spam emails for diet pills, devices that promise to lengthen certain appendages, and pleas from the daughter of a deceased African politician who requires assistance transferring $10 million from her clandestine bank account in Kinshasa.

Some signs we have seen before, others are simply too rude for publication, but around half of the pictures we receive are funny and fresh enough to make our weekly gallery. And, with the ever-growing dominance of English as the language of choice in most arenas around the world – from business and pop music to international diplomacy – combined with the rise of free online translators, the steady flow of photographs is unlikely to be stemmed any time soon.

Our dedicated army of camera-wielding readers has kept *Sign Language* going for more than 200 weeks and over the following pages we present our favourite submissions from the past year.

But what is it that makes the error-prone attempts of our foreign cousins to use the world's *lingua franca* so thoroughly enjoyable?

The very nature of the English language renders it an utter minefield for non-natives. As Bill Bryson points out in his excellent book *Mother Tongue* 'any language where the unassuming word fly signifies an annoying insect, a means of travel, and a critical part of a gentleman's apparel is clearly asking to be mangled'. Like the sport of cricket, it takes a lifetime of exposure to truly understand its nuances.

This complexity also allows for a depth of expression that is virtually unrivalled. No nation of comparable size can boast the same number of world-renowned poets, playwrights, authors and lyricists as Britain does. So perhaps it is a certain sense of superiority that enables us to laugh so heartily at these ham-fisted attempts to master the Queen's English. Would a Chinese speaker find the same amusement at the sight of a poorly drawn character, or a German guffaw over a missing umlaut?

The British sense of humour is also mired in word play. From irony and innuendo to riddles and limericks, we are a nation in love with the subtle use and misuse of our language. Get it right, and you've got Shakespeare, Dickens, Donne and Lennon. Get it wrong, and you've got the following gems. Fortunately, there is a time and place for both. Enjoy!

AT YOUR SERVICE

'Sale now on', 'New collection just in'. Shop fronts are there to entice us. To pull us from the street with promises of treasures within.

To the browsing tourist, however, they often conjure up rather less-than persuasive images. A seemingly winning name for a local business, when viewed through the eyes of a foreign visitor, can end up being unintentionally hilarious. What self-respecting woman wants to be seen sipping a latte under the sign of cafe Minga in Buenos Aires? And who would knowingly entrust their smalls to the care of India's Shitbra Laundry?

Of all businesses, hotels with humorous names appear to provide particular pleasure for the readers of *Sign Language*, and they've spotted many on their travels. We're sure that the majority of the establishments they photograph are fine places to stay, but the grubby sign above a row of bins declaring a Leicester bed and breakfast fit for the 'discerning traveller' is fooling no-one.

Similarly, if you have travelled all the way to Vietnam, are you really going to want to spend your precious local dong on a hotel called My Dung? Basil Fawlty, you have nothing to worry about.

For the holidaymaker in need, though, an unfortunate sign over an essential service can provoke worry rather than laughter. Take the Wong Kwee Mau Dentist in Malaysia, London's own Kings Cross Eye Clinic, or the brilliantly named Wright Hassall, a firm of solicitors near Warwick whose clients no doubt value their honesty.

DUMB WAITERS →
Location: Niagara Falls, USA
Spotted by: Tobias Reynolds

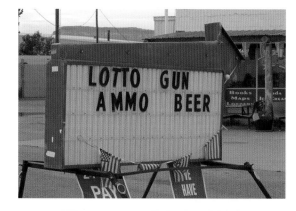

→ LUCKY SHOT
Location: South Dakota, USA
Spotted by: Tim Williams

→ COULD DO WITH A FACELIFT
Location: Buenos Aires, Argentina
Spotted by: Tobias

← MARKETING GURU REQUIRED
Location: Penang, Malaysia
Spotted by: David Freeman

↑ COWBOY BUILDERS
Location: Aurignac, France
Spotted by: Jonathan Benn

← BIT OF A HEAP
Location: Vietnam
Spotted by: Paul Lovelady

→ LAST HURRAH
Location: Minnesota, USA
Spotted by: Nick Drouet

→ HAIR TODAY, GONE TOMORROW
Location: Ulaanbaatar, Mongolia
Spotted by: Peter Smith

→ HAIR RAISING
Location: France
Spotted by: Jane Cromey-Hawke

← RISKY BUSINESS
Location: Malawi
Spotted by: Colin McCulloch

← **BLINKING USELESS**
Location: Kuala Lumpur, Malaysia
Spotted by: Andy Hollingworth

→ **CHEEKY DEALS**
Location: Warwick, UK
Spotted by: Kathryn Holton

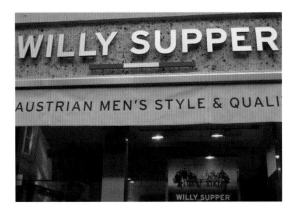

→ CHOW DOWN
Location: Graz, Austria
Spotted by: Richard Beardsall

→ HIS HANDS ARE FULL
Location: Newquay, UK
Spotted by: Tony Butler

← STUPORMARKET
Location: Isleworth, UK
Spotted by: Howard Hope

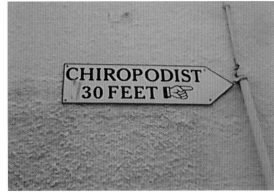

← **MAY LEAVE A TRAIL**
Location: Thailand
Spotted by: Adride Zwart

→ **WASH BEFORE USE**
Location: Darjeeling, India
Spotted by: Jeremy Smith

→ CAN BUY ME LOVE
Location: Norwich, UK
Spotted by: Hannah Gascoigne

→ TOURIST CRAP
Location: Bangkok, Thailand
Spotted by: Philip Hellawell

← DESTINED FOR DENTISTRY
Location: Melaka, Malaysia
Spotted by: Mike Noble

the kings cross eye clinic

280
zacks london eye clinics
WINNER OPTICIAN AWARDS
OPTOMETRIST OF THE YEAR

020 7713 7713   www.kcec.co.uk

← TRY OUR CHARING CROSS BRANCH
Location: London, UK
Spotted by: Peter Jenkinson

→ TOO MUCH TO HANDLE
Location: Reading, UK
Spotted by: Aaron Bebington

The KNOB SHOP

DOOR, WINDOW
& BATHROOM
FURNITURE

NET &
RICAL
INGS

→ ON THE TAKE
Location: Makkum, Friesland, Netherlands
Spotted by: Nigel Hand

→ LEGAL NIGHTMARE
Location: near Warwick, UK
Spotted by: Toby Warrington

← SURPRISE PARTING
Location: Manila, Philippines
Spotted by: Dwight D. Swanson

← **NOT WHAT THEY SEEM**
Location: Rome, Italy
Spotted by: Sonny Mallet

→ **POTTY POTTERY**
Location: Spain
Spotted by: Vic Sofras

CERAMICAS
ARSE

CERAMICA VALENCIANA. J. GIMENO

พร ซัก อบ รีด
PORN LAUNDRY

038-411286
ห้องเช่า
087-112-5897
ROOM FOR RENT

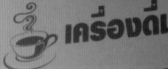 เครื่องดื่ม

DRINK

LEVITRA | VIAGRA

→ LITTLE AND LARGE
Location: Portivy, France
Spotted by: Eric Vlek

→ ROOMY
Location: Harbin, China
Spotted by: Tom Marshall

← DIRTY WASHING
Location: Pattaya, Thailand
Spotted by: Oliver Minto

← **MONEY LAUNDERING**
Location: Peru
Spotted by: Dick Hemphill

→ **CARAMEL AND CAPES**
Location: North Yorkshire, UK
Spotted by: Ian Braithwaite

the big ozzy clothing

FASHIONABLE CLOTHING
FOR THE LARGER MAN
2XL TO 8XL

COME AND SEE US
(NEXT TO THE CHOCOLATE FACTORY)

# HOMELESS
the life style store

17-19 yun ping rd.

→ OR, 'BIN AND BREAKFAST'?
Location: Leicester, UK
Spotted by: Peter Tomlinson

→ GLAZED OVER
Location: Banff, Aberdeenshire, UK
Spotted by: Jane Harris

← SHABBY CHIC
Location: Hong Kong
Spotted by: Tim Wong

NEW PAIN
TATTOO PIERCING

☎ 96 579 41 23

← TRUST ME, YOU WON'T FEEL A THING
Location: Costa Blanca, Spain
Spotted by: Peter Wood

→ THE REAL DEAL
Location: Ölüdeniz, Turkey
Spotted by: Mike Farrington

HERCULES TIRES

RIDE ON OURSTRENGTH.

MERTKOL LASTİK SERVİSİ

Tel:0392 821 33 22 - Cep:0533 851 89 29

→ RAISING THE STANDARD

Location: Panama City,
Republic of Panama
Spotted by: Stephen Gamester

→ BREAST AND RELAXATION

Location: Hudson Valley, USA
Spotted by: Sue Pallant

← NOT THE STUFF OF LEGEND

Location: Cyprus
Spotted by: John Naylor

← **THEY SAW YOU COMING**
Location: Mountain View, California, USA
Spotted by: Claudia Loyear

→ **SHOP 'TIL YOU POP**
Location: unknown
Spotted by: Richard Summerfield

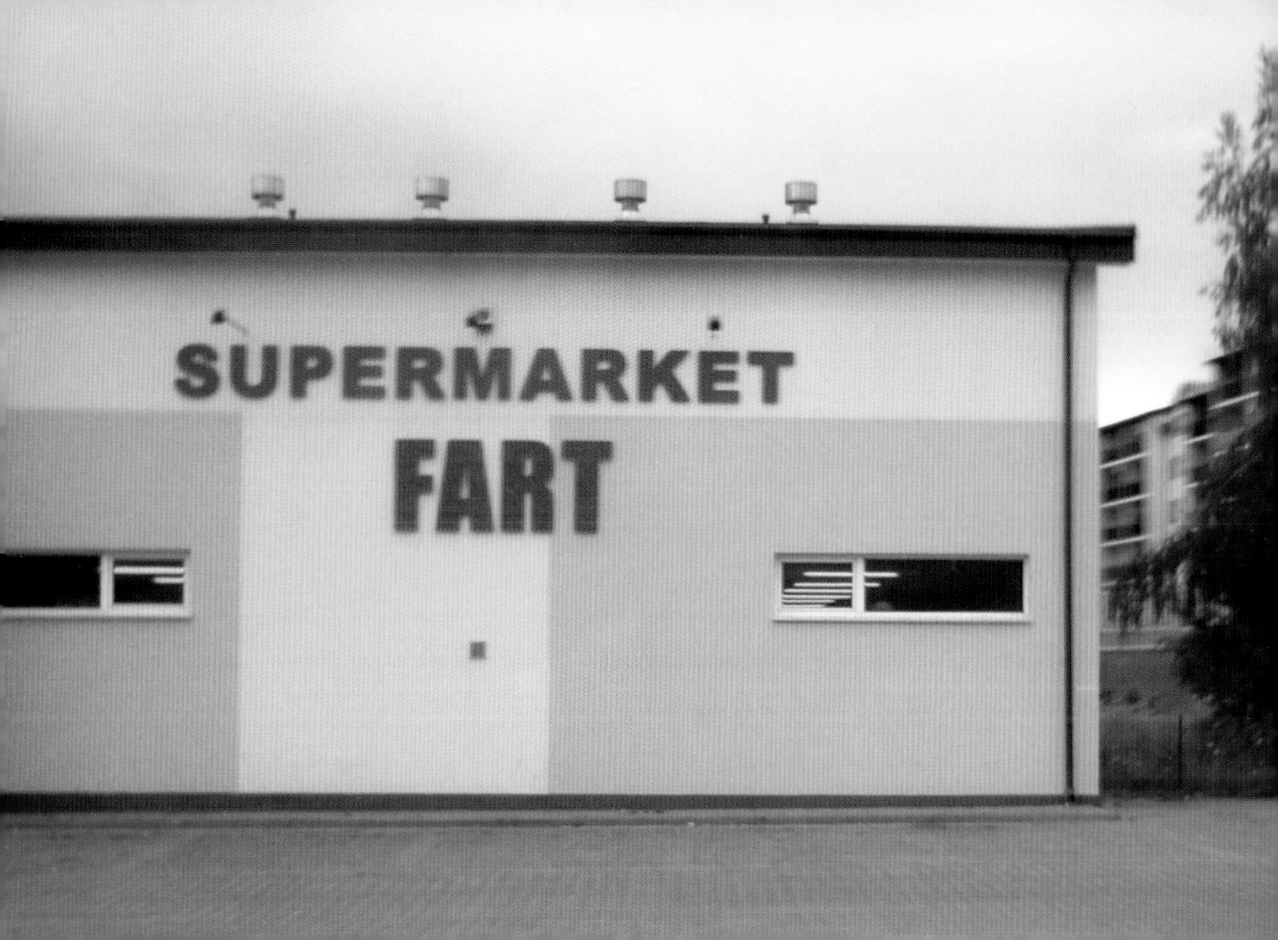
SUPERMARKET
FART

ON THE ROAD

They are meant to tell you where to go. Or warn you what lies ahead. Or tell you what you are looking at. And most signs you see on the road will do one of these. But the following stand out from the rest. They still let you know what's going on (well, mostly). It's just that their tone may pull you up short or make you guffaw.

Not that it's their fault. I mean, if a village is called Crackpot, then what's a sign to do other than point in its direction? And if someone in Hong Kong names their company Fook Kit Transportation, don't blame the innocent truck for those puerile Western tourists and their twisted word plays.

Other signs seen from behind the steering wheel may take you into the realm of the bizarre – a nonsensical and occasionally nightmarish world of roads prone to 'sudden catastrophic sinkhole collapses', crossings for 'humped puffins' and parking reserved for moose.

It's a strange old place indeed where street signs warn of 'no access to Magpies'. And what are we coming to when Jesus is 'for lease' – as one road-side offering in New Zealand inadvertently suggests? After a journey through these pages, your road trips may never be the same again.

YOUR NUMBER'S UP →
Location: Martin's Haven, Wales, UK
Spotted by: Julian Ward

→ LIFE'S A BEACH
Location: North Island, New Zealand
Spotted by: Dudley Chignall

→ A CLASS APART
Location: Barcelona, Spain
Spotted by: Gregor Carfrae

← YOU CAN SWEAR BY THEM
Location: Hong Kong
Spotted by: Catalina Magnusson

← TWINNED WITH DULL,
SCOTLAND
Location: Oregon, USA
Spotted by: Melanie Walton

→ THE SECOND COMING
Location: New Mexico, USA
Spotted by: Ron Simpson

ADULT
VIDEO
JESUS
IS WATCHING YOU
The Roman Catholic Churches of San Juan County

→ **PRIVATE ROAD**
Location: Lincolnshire, UK
Spotted by: Andy Pendegrass

→ **TOY GUNS**
Location: Scotland, UK
Spotted by: Vic Pommer

← **ROAD TO RUIN**
Location: Ladakh, India
Spotted by: Richard Lewis

FANNY HANDS LANE

01780 462355
sequencehome.co.uk

PISTOL MAKERS ROW

CAUTION Children Playing

← **MINI MADNESS**
Location: Toronto, Canada
Spotted by: Pete Morris

→ **THE TIP OF THE ICEBERG**
Location: Peru
Spotted by: Judith Cronin

TURISMO
TITANIC

LIMA-CHIMBOTE-TRUJILLO-CHEPEN-PACASMAYO-CHICLAYO- FERREÑAFE

→ **ESPECIALLY AT
BEAK TIMES**
Location: Nettlebed, Oxfordshire, UK
Spotted by: Mike Lewis

→ **NATIONAL SEXPRESS**
Location: Romania
Spotted by: Dan Sellers

← **ON SAFARI**
Location: Melbourne, Australia
Spotted by: Rachel Freeman

← ASHES TO SPLASHES
Location: Aldershot, UK
Spotted by: Anthony Radcliffe

→ MIXED MESSAGES
Location: Perth, Australia
Spotted by: Adam Beer

TOYOTA

HILUX
SR

UNJ·168

PREPARE
TO
STOP

NO
STOP PING

→ **DRAMMED IF YOU DO**
Location: India
Spotted by: Satnam Johal

→ **THAT SINKING FEELING**
Location: Alabama, USA
Spotted by: Mike Franklin

← **WHEELS ON FIRE**
Location: Seoul, South Korea
Spotted by: Richard Frampton

PARKING FOR *Drive Thru* CUSTOMERS ONLY

← SHOULD I STAY OR SHOULD I GO?
Location: Philippines
Spotted by: Bob Kaufman

→ PLEASE ADMIRE THE VIEW
Location: New Zealand
Spotted by: Simon Peakman

→ DOOR AND ORDER
Location: Didcot, UK
Spotted by: John Robinson

→ RIGHT OR WONG?
Location: Te Anau, New Zealand
Spotted by: David Todd

← FERRY SILLY
Location: Ross-shire, Scotland, UK
Spotted by: Hamish Champ

← **SENSITIVE SPOT**
Location: Germany
Spotted by: Alma Verbunt

→ **HIGHER PURCHASE**
Location: New Zealand
Spotted by: Stephen Helliwell

→ GET SERIOUS
Location: Silly, Belgium
Spotted by: Clare Pearson

→ WISH YOU WEREN'T HERE?
Location: Czech Republic
Spotted by: Richard Gibson

← DRY HUMOUR
Location: Nevada Desert, USA
Spotted by: John Woodard

← SURELY 'DENSELY POPULATED'?
Location: Sandwich, Cape Cod, USA
Spotted by: Andrew Abbott

→ SERVICE WITHOUT A SMILE
Location: Kuala Lumpur, Malaysia
Spotted by: Will Bathurst

→ BEDLAM AND BREAKFAST
Location: Yorkshire, UK
Spotted by: Les Crosthwaite

→ DO YOU COME HERE OFTEN?
Location: Slovakia
Spotted by: Dan Sellers

← FREAK OF NATURE
Location: Chesterfield, UK
Spotted by: John A. Grosvenor

← POSTIE TRAUMATIC STRESS DISORDER
Location: Omak, Washington, USA
Spotted by: Simon Farrow

→ CAR PARP
Location: Arizona, USA
Spotted by: Dave Shingledecker

→ DRIVEN MAD
Location: near Rye, East Sussex, UK
Spotted by: Gareth Owen

→ TOUCHED BY GOD
Location: North Waterboro, USA
Spotted by: Michael Rolfe

**← HEAVEN WELCOMES
CAREFUL DRIVERS**
Location: Bergun, Switzerland
Spotted by: Facundo Rosales

Foreign lavatories – from China's communal trenches to the hi-tech wizardry of a Japanese bowl – can be a real culture shock. Focusing on the task at hand is key, so the last thing you need is the distraction of unfathomable signs around you.

Rather than wondering why anyone would want to do their laundry in the toilet, just be grateful that the practice is prohibited. And on seeing the hurricane warning outside the men's toilets at Dallas-Fort Worth airport, assess not the importance of refried beans in a Texan's diet but complete your manoeuvre and proceed to your flight.

If you enjoy sampling the street food while travelling there is a chance you could be struck down with Delhi Belly. But for the backpackers frequenting Thai cafe Pee Soon, the name may, quite literally, be a sign of things to come.

Of course, for those poor globetrotters afflicted by problems down below, there are usually local remedies on offer. Although few can match the promise of Colombia's leading haemorrhoid cream, the dauntingly-branded NewAss.

As you may have guessed by now, what follows is nothing more than bog standard potty talk. But we think you'll like it.

TOILET HUMOUR

REGULAR GUSTS →
Location: Dallas-Fort Worth Airport, Texas, USA
Spotted by: John Bennett

SEVERE WEATHER AREA

MEN'S TOILET

WC

Vous êtes priés de ne pas jeter les couches des enfants ainsi que les serviettes hygiéniques dans les W.C.

Please don't throw the coats of the children as well as the sanitary towels in toilets.

← FEELING FLUSH
Location: France
Spotted by: B. Mallaby

↑ CUT THE CRAP
Location: China
Spotted by: Ron B

TOILET

← JEEPERS PEEPERS
Location: Indonesia
Spotted by: Rob Cullingworth

→ STOOL WATERS RUN DEEP
Location: school near Cardiff, UK
Spotted by: Stella Coombe

← Library
Llyfrgel

← Swim in Poo
Pwll Nofio

← Gymnasium
Campfa

← ATTACK OF THE KILLER TOMATOES
Location: Dubai
Spotted by: J. Wismark

↑ BOG STANDARD
Location: York, UK
Spotted by: Simon Dodge

ครัวพี่สุน ซีฟู๊ด
PEE SOON
ピースン

← **TRY THE 'DIURETIC DEL DIA'**
Location: restaurant in Koh Samui, Thailand
Spotted by: Mike Noble

→ **BUM NOTES**
Location: Veracruz, Mexico
Spotted by: Simon Chaplin

NOTICE

NO URINATING

VIOLATORS PHOTOGRAPH
WILL BE POSTED

Sign. Management

← FLASH PHOTOGRAPHY
Location: Jamaica
Spotted by: Kim deCasseres

↑ UNRESTRICTED MOVEMENT
Location: Nepal
Spotted by: Peter Nicholson

GOBBLEDEGOOK

noun: *meaningless or unintelligible language, especially when over-technical or pompous*

This chapter is reserved for those signs of such incomprehensibility that they could only derive from total reliance on an incompetently programmed online translator, or misplaced faith in the language skills of a raving lunatic.

We've received an awful lot of them during the past year, and they seem to have been spotted almost exclusively in the Far East – surely the world's foremost hotbed of gibberish and drivel? Most worryingly of all, these signs seem to rear their dangerously amusing heads wherever complete understanding is paramount – such as on a notice explaining fire evacuation procedure, or in the instructions for using a life raft.

Just imagine you were aboard a stricken ship, and found yourself tasked with making sense of the words 'enter to tube and hand, leg will control downing speed' or 'give a signal to outside and adjust the tube angle'. The expression 'sinking feeling' would barely do it justice.

CLOUD COVERAGE →
Location: Beijing, China
Spotted by: Mark Hughes

雷雨天气　请勿拨打手机

Thunderstorms do not call cell phones

~ Information ~

It will become, if it compares the in-and-out harbor from this harbor (Motohakone) by the unseasonable weather of a reed on the lake today. The ship plies from all facilities and the next Hakonemachi. * Please understand that I make trouble very much.

← NONSENSAURUS
Location: Cockatoo Island, Australia
Spotted by: Adam Beer

↑ TALKING SHIP
Location: Japan
Spotted by: Nicola Horton

服 务 项 目
Service item

俄罗斯小姐按	TheRussianyoungladymassage
全身保健按摩	Thewholebodycarestcmassage
男性性功能障	Walesexualfuntionobstacle
足底保健按摩	Thefootbottomcaresthemassage

代 开 发 票

↑ **AT YOUR SERVICE**
Location: calling card slipped under a hotel door in Kaifeng, China
Spotted by: Weronika Lesniak

→ **LOST IN TRANSLATION**
Location: China
Spotted by: Steve McDowall

The Binjiang Scenic Area Tour Notices

Binjiang Scenic Area is the window to show the culture and spiritual civilization of Guilin City. In order to maintain the environmental and safety, please follow below instruction during traveling:

1. Please purchase ticket in line and show it when entering the scenic. The Children who stature is below 1.4 meter and active army can enter the Scenic Area free when show related valid identification.

2. Pay attention on personal safety and property. Do not climb the rocks. Please do not stay in hill peah when have thunder storm weather.

3. Painting, carving and pasting at scenic area and historical sites is not allowed. Do not damage or rubbing the inscription.

4. Caring the scenic environment. The rubbish should be put into recycle bin. No spitting and no pissing at the public. The pet is not allowed to bring in.

5. Caring the plants. Keep off the grass. Do not put down and break off twigs or flowers.

6. No firing or smoking at public. It is forbidden take any kinds of guns, weapons, explosive items into the scenic.

7. Every body must obey the laws and rules. No fighting, no gambling, no any other illegal activities, such as superstition.

8. Only authorize car is allowed enter into scenic area.

9. Please cooperate with scenic staff and provide necessary assistance, in order to protect your benefit.

10. Please carry forward social democracy morality, civilization, civility, to be civilized tourist.

If Tourist need to complain or any other help, Please contact through this number: +86-(0)773-2100660. Scenic staff will provide to you our best services.

之地。为
秩序，特

出示入园

以防不慎
停留。
设施上涂

杂物；不

烟区内吸

不打架斗
禁在景区

和他人的

询投诉电

雨雪天气 小心滑跌

Rain and snow sliding down carefully

← **SNOW JOKE**
Location: Beijing, China
Spotted by: Mark Hughes

↑ **NOT LOST FOR WORDS**
Location: China
Spotted by: Peter Geldart

Please do not see it while drinking drink.

The PET bottle caps it and put it in a bag, and please carry it.
Please see the thing which the chief does not have after finishing

↑ **HAVE YOU BEEN DRINKING?**
Location: Kyoto , Japan
Spotted by: Stuart Lee

→ **CRUDE TUBE**
Location: South Korea
Spotted by: Patricia Ewing

터널식 구조대 사용방법
HOW TO USE TUNNEL TYPE LIFESAVING TUBE

(1) 화재시 창문을 먼저 해체하여 면적을 확보한다.
(1) BREAK THE WINDOW SO KEEP WELL LIFE-SAVING BAG WHEN FIRED.
(1) 火災時は 窓を こわして 救助袋の スペースを 確保 します。

(2) 4명이 1조가 되어 상자에서 구조대를 꺼내어 창문상단 고정핀에 파이프를 걸어 터널면직을
    확인 후 구조대를 창 밖으로 펼친다.
(2) 4 PEOPLE MAKES ONE TEAM., AT FIRST, TAKEN OUT LIFE-SAVING TUBE
    FROM BOX AND HANGING PIPE HANG TO WINDOW UPPER PIN APTER THEN
    THE TUBE THROW DOWN TO OUTSIDE.
(2) 4名が 一組となり 救助袋 を 箱より 取り 出し 窓上端の 固定ピンに パイフ を かけ
    て 救助袋 を 外側に 投出します。

(3) 창 밖 사람에게 신호하여 터널 구조대가 각도가 생기도록 고정한다.
(3) GIVE A SIGNAL TO OUTSIDE AND ADJUST THE TUBE ANGLE.
(3) 外部の 人に 知らせて 袋の 角度を 調整します。

(4) 탈출시 1명씩 누운자세로 터널속에서 팔, 다리를 펼쳐 속도를 조절하여 내려간다.
(4) EACH ESCAPER ENTER TO TUBE AND HAND, LEG WILL CONTROL DOWNING
    SPEED.
(4) 1名づつ 脱出の 事と 足と 腕にて 降下速度を 調節します。

(5) 먼저 탈출한 사람은 터널 구조대가 흔들리지 않도록 지상에서 협조한다.
(5) ESCAPED PEOPLE WILL HELP FOR LATER ESCAPER.

YOU DO NOT CONTINUE LOOKING!
Serve yourselfe your same the thorms of the bar.
They work out fresh, newly facts and are to eat.

1. It (he/she) takes a plate and meet taking (catching those that more you like).
2. When you end, do not throw (shoot) the tootpicks, leave them in the plate.
3. We will receive (charge) from you so many thorns as toothpicks have in the plate... and then we throw (add) account!

STATEMENT

柳の美

Our company is trademark of the chinese country note, is authori zed cambodian Phnom Penh shen Huaguo especially the trade Limited Company exclusive distribution to prevent the counterfe it to hold for the coffee stamps the entire color laser design, if do es not have the laser to adulterate the product, asks respectfully the consumer to clearly recognize the truth

cambodian exclusive distribution telephone:

077 85 1111 (~~012 368097~~
099 85 1111 ~~011 368097~~ cancel)

← **MAKING A MEAL OF IT**
Location: Tapas bar, Mallorca, Spain
Spotted by: Jacqueline Grimsley

↑ **WAKE UP AND SMELL THE COFFEE**
Location: Thailand
Spotted by: Adrianus Cornelis de Zwart

↑ GRASS NO LIKE
Location: Yunnan, China
Spotted by: Ray Pitt

→ A BIRD IN THE HAND
Location: China
Spotted by: Lois Freeke

留下文明美德，
带走美好记忆。

To leave with the memory,
please leave behind your virtue

优美环境靠大家，
废物随手放入箱。

As a beautiful environment is on all of us, please omnivorously put the waste in garbage can.

← LOSE YOURSELF IN THE MEMORIES
Location: China
Spotted by: Elaine Bailey

↑ TALKING RUBBISH
Location: China
Spotted by: Elaine Bailey

Holidays can be a risky business, especially for those of us who like a little culinary adventure on our travels. And while there are few pleasures that match chancing across a gorgeous hidden gem of a restaurant serving up fabulous local delicacies, sometimes such chance discoveries are best avoided.

The risk you take if you eat in Budapest's Fatâl Restaurant, for example, is plain to see, while the daily special of 'cholera' offered by an eatery in Bettmeralp, Switzerland, is only for those with iron constitutions. Waistlines, rather than lives, seem to be under threat at the Man Fat restaurant in Munich, while posteriors are in the firing line at a Texan burger joint serving the Big Az cheeseburger. But then the 'second-hand' food dished out by a restaurant in Luxembourg might be just the place to lose those few extra pounds.

Choosing to self-cater may seem like the safer option, but would you really want to slake your thirst with a can of Sweat in South Korea? Or how about nibbling on a nice bunch of 'testicles of mule' in Umbria, Italy? Perhaps you'd prefer a Knob bun in Helsinki, best accompanied by a tasty carton of Croatian Šlag?

Back to restaurants, then, and the myriad confusions thrown up by mistranslations on menus. 'Soup smell of urine' is enough to turn the strongest stomach, as would the 'curry of mini child', in Tokyo. Best to stick to the Fu King Gou restaurant in Kos, Greece, then. Just be sure to stay clear of the 'evil water'.

FOOD AND DRINK

RUMP →
Location: Ozona, Texas, USA
Spotted by: Lee H. Wilson

↑ GRAB A SPOON
Location: Virginia, USA
Spotted by: Jillian Page

→ NOODLE IN A HAYSTACK
Location: Birmingham, UK
Spotted by: Steve and Yvonne Douglas

← ... OR FOO KOFF!
Location: New York, USA
Spotted by: Stephen Foster

↑ HARD TO STOMACH
Location: Xi'an, China
Spotted by: Chris Parker

← BOTTOM FEEDERS
Location: Zurich, Switzerland
Spotted by: Andrea Tomlinson

→ OR ELSE!
Location: London, UK
Spotted by: Struan Robertson

品名： **芝 士 核 桃**

Brothers

产地：北京　等级：合格　价格：8 元　规格：／　单位：个　物价员：01

北京市发展和改革委员会监制 Z01－111

【特定原材料】

奶酪 & 核桃

Cheese & Semen juglandis

好兄弟の面包工房

1pic

￥ 8 元

↑ QUACK CRACK
Location: Honolulu, Hawaii, USA
Spotted by: Melanie Utu

→ PROMISCUOUS PUD
Location: Hvar, Croatia
Spotted by: Husam Fakhry

← I'LL PASS, THANKS
Location: Beijing, China
Spotted by: Rachael McGuinness

↑ INSIDE OUT
Location: Czech Republic
Spotted by: Derek Beggs

← SLEAZY SPOON
Location: Cotteridge, UK
Spotted by: Neil Appadu

→ LOST YOUR APPETITE?
Location: Ozdee, Turkey
Spotted by: Ben Arram

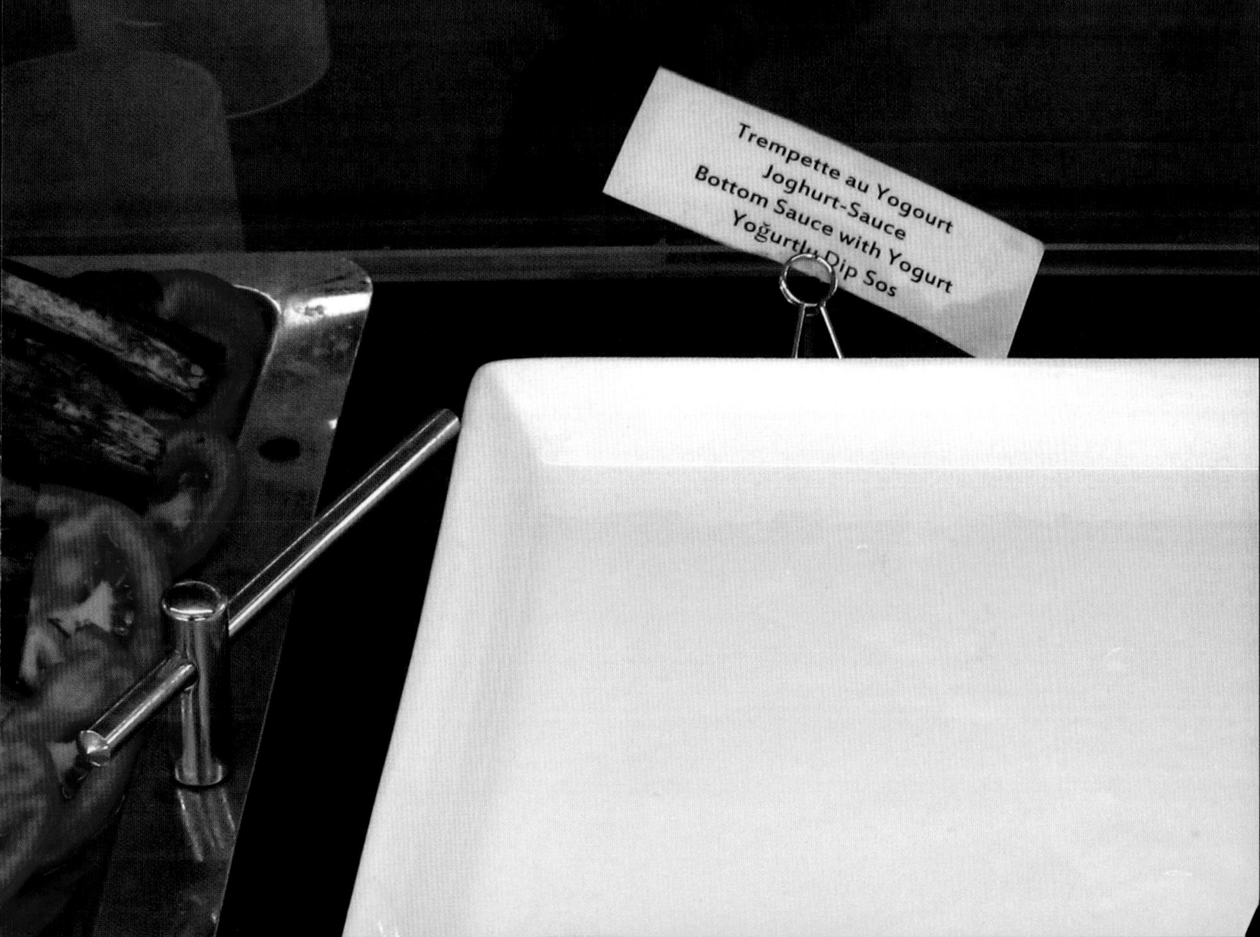

Trempette au Yogourt
Joghurt-Sauce
Bottom Sauce with Yogurt
Yogurtlu Dip Sos

好食道 餐厅 海派
Smart Norshery Makes You Slobber.

1028
南泉北路

MART NORSHERY MAKES YOU SLOBBER 好食道
年夜饭
火爆预订中

MART NORSHERY MAKES YOU

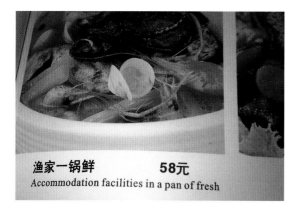

渔家一锅鲜　　　58元
Accommodation facilities in a pan of fresh

↑ **GIVE ME SHELLTER**
Location: Pudong, Shanghai, China
Spotted by: Paul Edwards

→ **TAKES THE BISCUIT**
Location: Osaka, Japan
Spotted by: Catalina Magnusson

← **MOUTH-WATERING**
Location: China
Spotted by: Lois Freeke

**↑ USED PIZZA SEEKS
CAREFUL EATER**
Location: Luxembourg
Spotted by: Graham Chambers

← SERF AND TURF
Location: Knebworth,
Hertfordshire, UK
Spotted by: Dave Hill

→ GOURMET GONADS
Location: Umbria, Italy
Spotted by: G.B. Aicardi

CASARECCIO SUL QUALE VA SPALMATO IL LARDO
MANGIATO PREFERIBILMENTE A SPICCHI.

Norcia
coioni di mulo
testicles of mule
hoden vom maultier
€/cad 7.00

palle del nonno
granfathers testicles
hoden des grossvaters
€/cad 7.00

proso
mini
mini
€/

String-tied trip sausage, *chips* _____

Chicken breast *with Aravis cream sauce, reblochon chees*

Tartiflette, *cured ham, salad* _____

Beef carpaccio, *chips and salad* _____

Chef's dick confit, *fried potatoes* _____

Choice of sauce: *béarnaise, pepper, roquefort chees*

SIDE DISHES

Chips _____ 4,50

Baked potatoes _____ 4,50

↑ **I COULDN'T EAT
A WHOLE ONE**
Location: Helsinki, Finland
Spotted by: Douglas Duncan

→ **BABY FOOD**
Location: Tokyo, Japan
Spotted by: Trevor Smith

← **HE LIKES TO THROW
HIMSELF INTO HIS WORK**
Location: Annecy, France
Spotted by: Ian Riches

Frozen Vegetarian

↑ MAY CONTAIN BONES
Location: Taipei, Taiwan
Spotted by: Catalina Magnusson

← CANNED HEAT
Location: Ulsan, South Korea
Spotted by: Alan E. Matthews

→ CURDS AND ... WAHEY!
Location: Oberstdorf, Germany
Spotted by: David Jones

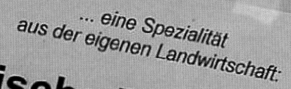

... eine Spezialität
aus der eigenen Landwirtschaft:

frische Dickmilch

naturgesäuert
mit Früchten, Zimtzucker, Brot oder Bratkartoffeln

↑ BEIJING BELLY
Location: Beijing, China
Spotted by: Nick Buckenham

→ CATCH IT WHILE YOU CAN
Location: Bettmeralp, Switzerland
Spotted by: Neil Jones

← ALL YOU CAN EAT
Location: Munich, Germany
Spotted by: Mark Morritt

12-10 依云水
Evil Water

30.00/60.00¥
Small/Big

↑ SOURCED FROM THE STYX?
Location: China
Spotted by: Lois Freeke

← THE LAST SUPPER
Location: Budapest, Hungary
Spotted by: Jon Greenwood

→ IT'S ALL GREEK TO ME
Location: Kos, Greece
Spotted by: Lucian Comoy

RESTAURANT
FU KING GOU
INTERNATIONAL
Traditional GREEK
CHINESE

FU KING GOU

NATURE

Cruelty to animals is no laughing matter. We are British after all, and famed for our love of all creatures, great and small. But even animal-loving *Sign Language* fans can't help but giggle at the Australian sign that cheerfully reads, 'We can shoot your pets and you can hang them on your wall!'

Nor can we suppress a chuckle at the inappropriately named Wild Freedom Taxidermy, in South Africa. And who could keep a straight face at the picnic sign in Illinois which seems to recommend random brutality by declaring, 'To aid your enjoyment, please eliminate dogs'?

But even us nature-loving Britons must accept that animal rights can be taken too far. Is irritating an animal best punished by the amputation of a limb? Yes, if the sign at a crocodile park in South Africa is anything to go by. Here, if a visitor shows any sign of bothering a croc, they are given short shrift: throw litter into a crocodile pen and you're told to go in and retrieve it yourself.

Here at home, in Norfolk, monkeys seem to be given the same road-crossing rights as children, according to at least one sign. And across the Irish Sea a Dublin zoo instructs visitors to refrain from climbing on the fences – not to protect themselves, mind, but because if they fall in to the enclosures and are eaten, they might make the animals sick.

Japan – perhaps unsurprisingly – takes it to extremes. Saunter into any supermarket and you'll see the ultimate catnip, the treat to end all treats: Cat Smack. Drug rehabilitation for Moggy, anyone?

MORE ADDICTIVE →
THAN CATNIP
Location: Japan
Spotted by: Jenny Norman

WARNING

Tree worrying is
an offence.
Sheep caught
will be shot.

→ FLIPPIN' ELK!
Location: Tillamook, Oregon, USA
Spotted by: Charles Bellinger

→ TWITCHER'S HUMOUR
Location: unknown
Spotted by: John Adams

← BAA-RKING UP THE WRONG TREES
Location: Forest of Bowland, Lancashire, UK
Spotted by: Tim Bridgeman

← **DODGE CITY**
Location: Albacete, Spain
Spotted by: Eloy Cebrian

→ **MOGSHOT**
Location: Australia
Spotted by: Chris Hall

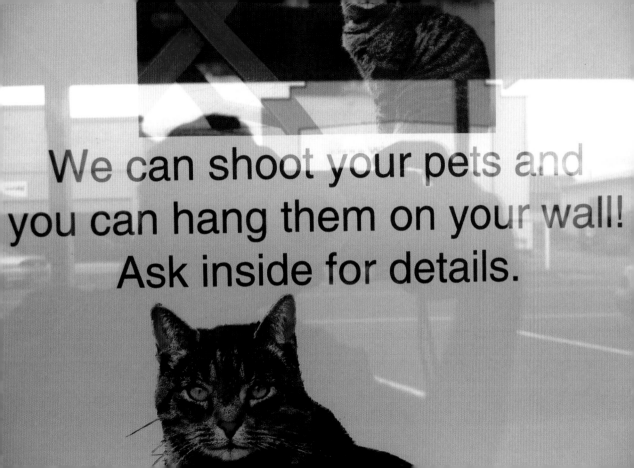

→ BLANKET WARNING
Location: Benbecula, Outer Hebrides, UK
Spotted by: Gillian Oakes

→ GET STUFFED
Location: South Africa
Spotted by: Michael Rolfe

← MONKEY BUSINESS
Location: Aylsham, Norfolk, UK
Spotted by: Kenneth Pantling

NOTICE

DOG WASTE BAGS ARE PROVIDED FOR USE ON THIS FOUNDATION PROPERTY ONLY.

PLEASE DO NOT TAKE THESE BAGS FOR YOUR PERSONAL USE.

YOUR COOPERATION IS APPRECIATED.

Nantucket Conservation Foundation, Inc.
Post Office Box 13

← **BAG IT UP**
Location: Nantucket, Massachusetts, USA
Spotted by: Adam Hewitt

→ **RUMBLE IN THE JUNGLE**
Location: Dublin Zoo, Ireland
Spotted by: Gemma Tremlett

Do not stand, sit, climb or lean on zoo fences. If you fall, animals could eat you and that might make them sick. Thank you.

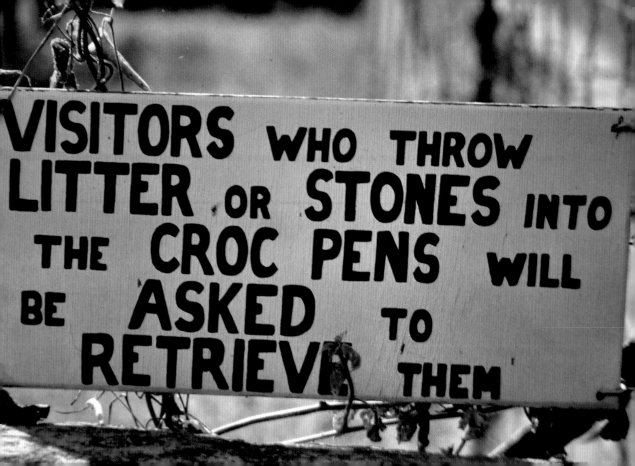

→ ROVER AND OUT
Location: Evanston, Illinois
Spotted by: Nick Hum

→ HITHER SLITHER
Location: Arizona, USA
Spotted by: Colin Walker

← CROC OFF
Location: South Africa
Spotted by: Keith Hughes

Once a week at *Telegraph Travel* HQ, as we pick through the best of readers' *Sign Language* submissions, a bitter war is waged between decency and comedy. Needless to say, it is the latter that usually prevails. How else would one explain the presence of these gratuitously puerile signs on the website of a family newspaper like the *Telegraph*?

Despite the best efforts of the more conservative minds on the desk, Señor Dick's bar and restaurant has been showcased in our respected publication, as has rival establishment Willy's Hang-Out. And only the quest for immature giggles could possibly explain the presence of the Fourskin boutique, the Kiek in de Kök museum and the Dildo Trading Post of Newfoundland on our hallowed pages.

For those readers who feel that *Sign Language* should be kept pure, high-brow and smut-free, we invite you to register your opposition. For more information on our complaints procedure, see www.ank-tours.ch.

X-RATED

A BIT OF A DING-DONG →
Location: Taipei, Taiwan
Spotted by: Catalina

小叮噹科學主題樂園

LITTLE DING-DONG SCIENCE PARK

المدينة

M AD A NAL PLAZA

← CRAZY ASS SQUARE
Location: Muscat, Oman
Spotted by: James Miller

↑ A GREAT PLACE TO HANG OUT
Location: Newquay, UK
Spotted by: Chris Seagrave

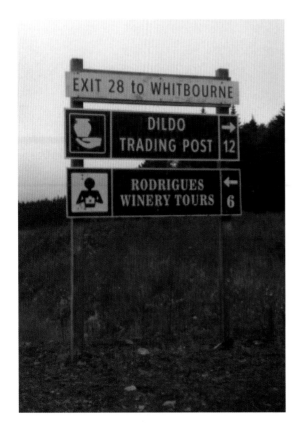

← **BUSINESS AND PLEASURE**
Location: Newfoundland, Canada
Spotted by: James Loder

→ **COME AND STAY**
Location: Germany
Spotted by: Jonathan Card

"WE HOPE YOU ENJOY YOUR STAY"

GUEST TO NOTE

PLEASE BREAKFAST IS SERVED FROM MONDAY TO SUNDAY OUTSIDE YOUR ROOMS

TIME   : 7AM – 10AM

VENUE : BAR, RESTURANT OR ON THE COMPOUND OF THE HOTEL PREMISES.

             PLEASE BE PUNCTUAL AT THE ALLOCATED VENUE.

YOU DO NOT HAVE TO WORRY WHEN YOU COME UNPREPARED
FOR WE ARE HERE TO HELP YOU DRIVE SAFELY WITH A
SILICONE LUBRICATED NATURAL LATEX CONDOM FOR ONLY
GH¢2.00. SAFE RIDE…SAFE JOURNEY WITH WHITE WATER CONDOM.

YOU CAN MAKE YOUR PURCHASE AT THE RECEPTION 24/7

THANK YOU

BY MANAGEMENT

← DRIVEN TO DISTRACTION
Location: Accra, Ghana
Spotted by: Geoffrey Mugan

↑ SELF SERVICE
Location: restaurant in Colindale, London, UK (now closed)
Spotted by: Suzanne Grant

← **WOODWORK**
Location: Furniture shop, Deventer, the Netherlands
Spotted by: Eric Vlek

→ **TWO FOR THE PRICE OF ONE**
Location: Phuket, Thailand
Spotted by: Keith Blacker

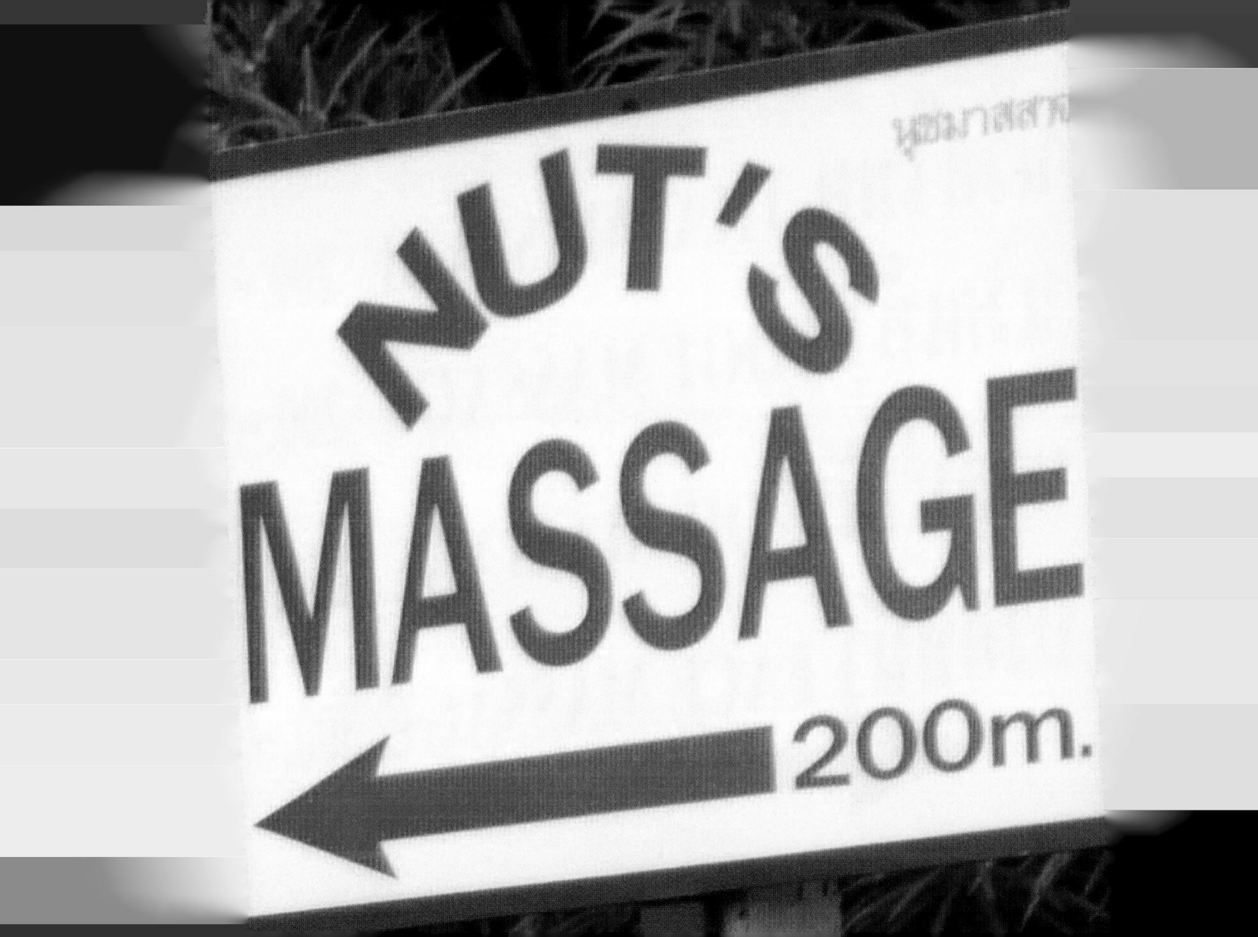
NUT'S
MASSAGE
200m.

**← GET A FEEL FOR
THE REGION
Location:** Switzerland
Spotted by: Alastair Miller

**↑ A SWINGING PLACE
Location:** Pattaya
Spotted by: Pennie Uygurer

Spunk Trouser

Flat

30%

Off

← **ARE THEY WIPE CLEAN?**
Location: Darjeeling, India
Spotted by: Jeremy Smith

→ **FORM AN ORDERLY QUEUE**
Location: Copenhagen, Denmark
Spotted by: Henry Clappison

BLAND SELV SLIK

OVER
300 SLAGS

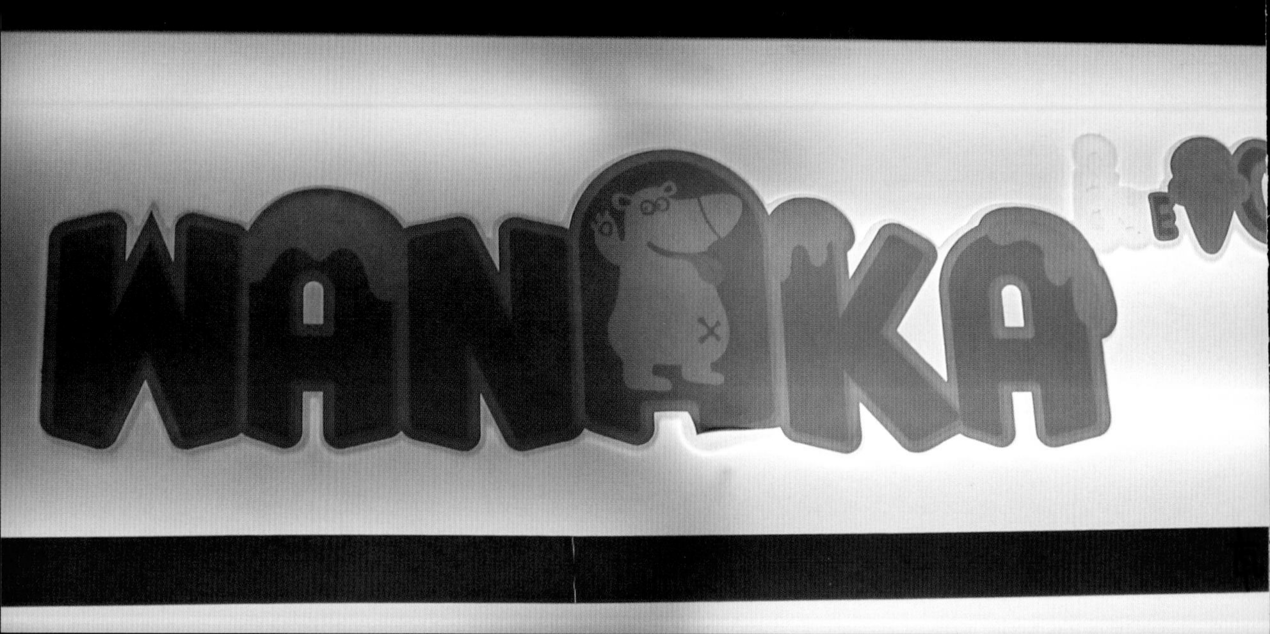
WANAKA

← WE PREFER MR WHIPPY
Location: Shanghai
Spotted by: Roger Rosewarne

↑ DIY
Location: Japan
Spotted by: Samantha Moran

VOORDEEL VOORDEEL

Albert Heijn

PANTY MOUSSE

matterend effect
versterkt broekje

4 stuks

20 denier

42-44
Hazel

← **KNICKERBOCKER GLORY**
Location: Rotterdam, the Netherlands
Spotted by: Jonathan Wheeler

→ **ONE SIZE FITS ALL**
Location: Singapore
Spotted by: Andrew McCarthy

← JOIN THE QUEUE
Location: Tokyo, Japan
Spotted by: Keith Hughes

↑ ALL THE WRONG SIGNALS
Location: Gökova, Turkey
Spotted by: Robert Pearson

← FRUITY
Location: Vire, Normandy, France
Spotted by: Jonathan Lowth

→ NO. 1 AND NO. 2
Location: Thun, Switzerland
Spotted by: Paul Bingley

DIC HELMET

www.dic-helmet.co.jp

Cプラスチック株式会社 　製造元 DICモールディング株

← **SAFETY FIRST**
Location: Tokyo, Japan
Spotted by: Mark Harewood

↑ **HANDLE WITH CARE**
Location: Bath, UK
Spotted by: Richard Miller

← **MUSEUM OF PAIN**
Location: Tallinn, Estonia
Spotted by: Mick Fawcett